RAJARSI JANAKANANDA (JAMES J. LYNN)

American self-made business magnate
who became an illumined yogi

RAJARSI JANAKANANDA

(James J. Lynn)

A Great Western Yogi

SELF-REALIZATION FELLOWSHIP

Publishers

Los Angeles, California

1984

Authorized by the International Publications Council of Self-Realization Fellowship

ISBN-0-87612-182-2

Printed in the United States of America

10462-54321

CONTENTS

Rajarsi Janakananda

(James J. Lynn)

Rajarsi Janakananda

(JAMES JESSE LYNN)

May 5, 1892—February 20, 1955

Revered president, 1952-1955, of Self-Realization Fellowship of America and Yogoda Satsanga Society of India.

Ideal disciple of Paramahansa Yogananda for more than twenty-three years.

A LITTLE BIRTHDAY GIFT

By Paramahansa Yogananda

(*Written for Rajarsi in 1939 on his birthday, May 5th*)

Into the cradle of my love
Came a little one from above:
An image of love divine,
Of humbleness, understanding, will adamantine.

That day the earth was blessed:
An ideal child adorned her breast,
To be an example after my dreams;
To know and show others: "Earth is not what it seems."

The saintly little one, sitting
On an altar of grass, meditating;
Enshrined by a temple of sky and sun,
Thinking of only one — the Only One.

Could more joy I feel
Than in beholding his soul with the seal
Of mine own and the Great Ones' complete content,
In this path of divine intent?

When such a one awoke in God's love
Flowers unseen rained from above
Not here only; but in the lightland
Of India, blessed by the Astral Dove.

Rajarsi Janakananda outside the Self-Realization Fellowship Hermitage,
Encinitas, California, 1951

The Life of James J. Lynn

By DICK FOWLER

Reporter, "Kansas City Star," Kansas City, Missouri

(The following biography, reprinted by permission of the "Kansas City Star," Kansas City, Missouri, was published in that newspaper on May 13, 1951. The article was later included in "Leaders In Our Town," a book by Mr. Fowler on the lives of prominent Kansas Citians.)

At nine o'clock on the morning of the ninth day of the ninth month in the year 1909 a homesick seventeen-year-old youth named Jimmy Lynn got off the train at the old Union Depot. Perhaps even then the something different in his nature was coming to the surface, something that caused him to notice the coincidence of the number 9.

Although the day was Sunday, he walked across the railroad tracks to the Missouri Pacific office above the freight house. Men were working, so he went to work.

Some twelve years later the whole business community of Kansas City knew James J. Lynn, successor to U. S. Epperson, and owner (with a huge debt) of the insurance underwriting company for a large share of the lumber industry. He stood out as a youthful prodigy.

Builder of a "Business Empire"

This year, 1951, people who like the ring of the term "business empire" could put Mr. Lynn in the empire class, at least by Kansas City standards. It spreads into three separate insurance operations, and into oil production, citrus fruits, railroading, and a substantial banking interest. Financially the original Epperson enterprise is now overshadowed by oil, but it is the largest reciprocal fire exchange in the world.

This man who pushes ahead, building and expanding in the world of big business, is unique. In one sense he suggests a mystic in Babylon, a man more concerned with a religious philosophy than with any of the showy or luxurious things that money can buy.

Life Close to Nature

His private office in the R. A. Long Building breathes financial stability: a massive walnut office hung with heavy draperies in the

11

manner of past decades. The bald man behind the heavy desk is bronzed from persistent living outdoors. Life close to nature is part of his creed. His face is so sensitive that you hardly notice the square jaw. There is nothing about him to suggest the bulldog type....

The scope of his activities implies that he is one of the busiest executives in this part of the United States. From this intensely practical life he takes time out for meditation; contemplates the meanings of humanity in the vast scheme of things. Out of these meditations and years of Bible reading and reading from other religions he has developed his own approach to the Christian philosophy. He discusses it freely, but not in a way that is easy for a visitor to understand. Superficially you can say it is wrapped up with the physical and mental side of daily living close to nature. To this writer it suggests a return to the simplicity of Christianity in earlier times when people worshipped in the forests.

The exercises which he takes outdoors (breathing, tensing, and relaxing exercises) may have been suggested by his reading of Oriental religions. This line of study started with a book by E. Stanley Jones, the famous missionary in Asia.[1]

An Estate of Forest and Orchards and Vineyards

Most Kansas Citians have driven past the 100-acre Lynn estate which lies between Sixty-third Street, Meyer Boulevard, and Paseo and Prospect. For years people have mentioned it in connection with his nine-hole golf course. The golf course was abandoned some years ago.

Beyond the fences and the shelter of dense foliage lie a forest and orchards and vineyards. This is James J. Lynn's outdoor retreat from early spring to late fall. He stays close to the orchards from the early flowering time to the season of harvest, and glows over the opportunity to give away fruits. In the forest are some 2,000 fine hardwood trees which antedate the encroachment of Kansas City. Winters he spends all possible time in southern California where he can continue to live outdoors.

This is the type of life Mr. Lynn manages to find in the midst of the business hurly-burly. While he is nominally vacationing in California he dashes back and forth to business meetings and the large conventions of lumbermen or automobile dealers, the men of the fields where he operates with insurance.

---

[1]One of the first books on Indian philosophy read by Mr. Lynn was a volume by Mr. Jones, but Mr. Lynn said that he was introduced to Hindu thought through an English translation of the Bhagavad-Gita. — *Editor.*

Mr. Lynn at the site of one of his oil wells, Archer City, Texas, 1950. The J. J. Lynn Oil Division was then in charge of about 25,000 acres of leases in Illinois, Oklahoma, Kansas, and Texas.

World's Largest Reciprocal Fire Insurance Exchange

His business for the lumber industry has multiplied itself many times to hold the rank of largest reciprocal fire exchange in any industry in the world. His somewhat similar type of reciprocal insurance for American motorcar dealers is not far behind; and within the last eighteen months he has launched a new stock company with full coverage for motorcar owners. It approached the million-dollar mark its first year and appears to be going far beyond that in 1951.

This man absorbed with things of the spirit is a very active oil man. His operations spread over some 25,000 acres of leases in Illinois, Kansas, Oklahoma, and Texas. Financially oil is the biggest of his enterprises, with a gross income from wells that now averages around two million dollars a year.

In the Rio Grande valley of Texas he is a large grower of citrus fruits, with 500 acres in grapefruit and orange groves. As the result of a freeze last January there will be no fruit from the area for two years. But in good times the income from 500 acres has run as high as a half-million dollars in a year.

A railroad job brought him to Kansas City and he is a railroad man today, one of the small group of Mid-Westerners who moved to gain control of the Kansas City Southern and the Louisiana and Arkansas railroads from Eastern interests and to lodge the headquarters firmly in Kansas City.

He is a banker: a very large stockholder and the chairman of the executive committee of the Union National Bank.

And this is the man spiritually akin to ancient prophets. Men of a slant only a shade different from his came out of the desert to denounce the splendor and wealth of Babylon.

One of the "Success Stories, Yet Different From Most"

The business rise of Jimmy Lynn is one of the most sensational American success stories, yet different from most. From the beginning, his talents have been carried by a peculiarly sensitive human being, one who could never bear the thought of any man's ill will.

He was born in 1892 near the crossroads village called Archibald, Louisiana. That long after the Civil War and the reconstruction period, the catastrophe still gripped the family.

Until Jimmy was six, his father was a tenant farmer. Jesse W. Lynn, a neat man with a blond mustache, worked hard to make up for all that had been lost. In the war the family had lost all its lands and slaves. Grandfather Lynn had died from a wound received in the Confederate

James J. Lynn at fourteen (*left*) and at seventeen. At fourteen he left home to make his own way in the world. He got an education, while holding full-time auditing positions, by attending evening classes in high-school subjects, accounting, and law. He passed the bar examinations at 21, and at 24 was a C.P.A. James Jackson of the *Kansas City Star* writes: "Mathematicswise, Lynn's IQ would have rung the bell for genius."

army. Jesse Lynn had never been given the chance even for normal education.

Eventually the family came into possession of a 120-acre farm that had been salvaged by Jimmy's mother's family, the Archibalds. And that farm was held under a debt to the other heirs.

Jimmy, the fourth of six children, took his turn chopping and picking cotton, but he was the member of the family assigned to help his mother whenever she needed him. She was a dark-eyed little woman, packed with energy; Scotch Presbyterian and saving. Most of Mr. Lynn's memories of his parents are of the hours working by their sides. There was seldom time for relaxation. He still gets pecans from the trees he and his mother set out on the farm.

His first reputation as a prodigy came at the age of five. That was the year he went to the little log schoolhouse two miles away. He was too young to receive much attention from the teacher, so he memorized everything in the Blue Back Speller.

One of the storekeepers at Archibald stood him on a cracker barrel to spell and give definitions, to the amazement of the loafers. Anything in the book — big words like "incompatibility" and "incomprehensible" —he spelled and rattled off the definitions of.

"Well, I swan!" and "I'll be a salted dog!" said the wise men of the corner-store crowd. [When he was a little older] he sat on the porch of this same store, selling fruit from the farm. Butter, he delivered to regular customers who had no cows of their own.

A Good Ball Player

His timidity and horror of causing displeasure may have helped his school record. He was shunted around from school to school, to whatever district could afford a teacher that year. And in each, the teacher pointed out Jimmy as an example of top classwork and perfect deportment. He saved himself from the label of "teacher's pet" in baseball. The first game in which the Archibald boys were outfitted in regular baseball suits, they beat the older Mangham town school-team 10 to 2. Jimmy scored four of the runs.

"On His Own" at the Age of Fourteen

The years Jimmy Lynn worked for the Missouri Pacific Railroad were unusual for one thing: when jobs were hard to get there was always a station agent who wanted him. He started at the Archibald station in school time, sweeping out and keeping the freight house in order for $2 a month. At fourteen and graduated from grammar school, he had a job at the Mangham railroad station and made his board and room

Mr. Lynn in 1937

James Lynn at age of twenty-one

doing chores at his cousin's hotel.

His first life ambition was fixed on the glamorous office of division superintendent, a life goal that he never achieved. The most impressive figure he knew was W. C. Morse, the division superintendent. In a private car this stern but warmhearted individual of knitted eyebrows traveled up and down the line. Whenever another station agent asked for Jimmy, Morse grumbled that Jimmy was too young, and always let him go.

That was the way he went to Oak Ridge for a temporary job at $35 a month. From there he moved on to Ferriday, the city and division point, at a remarkable $65 a month. When there was a second opening he got the job for his older brother, who married on the strength of it. Slackening business forced a cutback; Jimmy insisted that he was footloose and the one who should go. A traveling auditor for the road was quick to recommend him to a friend with the M. K. & T. railroad at Moberly, Missouri, and that turned out to be the highroad to Kansas City.

Homesickness can be a terrible thing for anyone. More than most teen-agers, Jimmy Lynn depended on the warmth and good feeling of human relations. At Moberly he was lost in a world of old people —old men at the office and two old women who rented him a room. One of these women struggled with music lessons and hammered away on the piano until all hours of the night. Then she resented Jimmy's alarm clock that went off early in the morning.

And so he found the job in Kansas City, working for the chief clerk to the Missouri Pacific division engineer. This chief clerk was a man he had known back in Louisiana. From that Sunday of his arrival in Kansas City he felt that he was among friends. Within a little more than seven years he was to be the general manager of the big underwriting company, second only to U. S. Epperson himself.

Promotions came fast. He was employed on the Missouri Pacific in Kansas City as an assistant auditor. In less than a month the auditor was transferred, and a frightened seventeen-year-old Jimmy Lynn handled the auditor's job. He learned it by doing the work and after that he was not afraid of new jobs.

Law School, High School — and a Full-Time Job

But the main theme of the seven years was education. He started from a public school education that had been cut off in the middle of the ninth grade.

About a year and a half after he had come to Kansas City a young assistant planted the idea of getting a legal education at the Kansas City school of law.

The law school exacted Jimmy Lynn's promise to make up the high-school education that he had missed. He carried his full law-school course and high-school subjects at the same time. Within a year he added a correspondence course in accounting to the load — sopped up education in three different fields by night and held a full-time job by day.

At twenty-one, before he had completed his law course, he was admitted to the bar. By that time he had stepped up to become an assistant in the firm of Smith & Brodie, certified public accountants.

Without such items as getting a high-school education and going through law school, Jimmy Lynn's accounting education alone would have been a prodigious undertaking. Two local accountants offered night courses to the correspondence school students, and Jimmy took them. On his own he read everything in accounting he could find and worked out all the problems.

Passed C.P.A. Examination, Highest Grade on Record

Under the rules of the state board, nobody could become a certified public accountant before the age of twenty-five. Long before that age Jimmy Lynn was handling involved, top-bracket accounting jobs for Smith & Brodie. When he was twenty-four he passed the state examination with the highest grade on record to that time. Confronted with such evidence the board waived the age rule and gave him his C.P.A. certificate at twenty-four. By that time he had a twenty percent interest in the [accounting] firm.

It was during this period of high-pressure education that Jimmy Lynn met and courted Miss Freda Josephine Prill of Kansas City. They were married in October, 1913.

Along with the urge to please everybody, Jimmy Lynn seems to have been born with unusual curiosity. It was his nature to look for the explanations of everything. For a curious individual, accounting can be an exciting adventure. Figures tell the story of a business, how it operates, and what makes it tick.

In Kansas City young Lynn was assigned to accounting work for the U. S. Epperson Underwriting Company and the Lumbermen's Alliance which it serves. In Chicago and St. Louis he audited other reciprocal insurance exchanges. The figures were business education....

Lynn Investigated with a Typical Thoroughness

Circumstances brought together the boyish Jimmy Lynn and the weighty Epperson. Lynn was assigned to audit the affairs of a burned-out Mississippi mill which happened to be a case that had particularly concerned U. S. Epperson. On the way to Mississippi, Lynn read Epperson's voluminous file and made a point of answering all the questions that had been raised. His audit revealed a clear motive for arson. Epperson showed that he was impressed. It happened at a critical time.

Death took H. A. Thomsen, the underwriting company's general manager, and Epperson was like a man who had just lost his right hand. He called on Lynn to straighten out some of his personal affairs, then offered him the job of treasurer in the company. Lynn refused.

Late at night, while he worked over the books in this office, Jimmy Lynn felt Epperson's eyes on him. And from time to time he heard the words, "I wish you weren't so young."

Out of that situation came an offer of the top job of general manager. At the age of twenty-four, barely arrived at the status of C.P.A., Jimmy Lynn had the experience of competing powers bidding for him. Epperson started with an offer of $5,000 a year and worked it up to an arrangement that amounted to $12,000. The salary was so precedent-shaking that Lynn was sworn to secrecy and it has been a secret to this time. Fred A. Smith, head of the accounting firm, countered by offering Lynn a full partnership which was probably worth more than Epperson's $12,000.

It wasn't salary that tipped the scales but opportunity. Epperson spoke of his age and of the chance to take full responsibility within a very few years. The opportunity turned out to be greater than Jimmy Lynn knew, and also far more precarious.

The hope of some day taking over full management for Epperson ended in 1921; Epperson decided to sell. He was ill and fearful that something would occur to destroy the value of his business. He wanted to put his affairs in order.

A frantic Jimmy Lynn proposed that he should buy the business himself. Epperson stated the very obvious fact, "You don't have the money."

A Risky Loan that Produced Great Results

In his later years E. F. Swinney, head of the First National Bank, talked about Jimmy Lynn as his No. 1 example of a risky loan that produced great results. Swinney elaborated with the enthusiasm of a man who might have been criticized or kidded for his daring.

The size of the loan which was the purchase price of the company has never been made public. It stood somewhere high in the hundreds of thousands and it was made strictly on the character of a young man who was not yet thirty years old. The notes were handled through the bank, but it was generally understood that Swinney had personally guaranteed the loan.

(LEFT) Mr. Lynn at the age of twenty-nine, when he became the owner of U.S. Epperson Underwriting Co. (RIGHT) Mr. Lynn in his Kansas City office, about 1937. "If we are at peace within our beings, we can harmoniously carry on our duties even in the business sphere," Mr. Lynn said. "We can accomplish admirable things in the world without necessarily clashing with others. Eventually we can perform all our duties with the full consciousness of God's presence."

When Lynn produced a check for the full amount of the purchase price, U. S. Epperson was so dumbfounded that he took a month to decide to accept the check and sign the contract.

The Epperson Company had originated with a problem in the lumber industry. Because of the fire hazards at lumber mills in early years they were unable to get insurance for more than three fourths their value and that only at exorbitant rates. In 1905 R. A. Long and other leaders of the industry organized the Lumbermen's Underwriting Alliance which was set up to spread the individual's risk throughout many companies in the industry, the group standing ready to make up the fire losses of any one [of the members]. U. S. Epperson formed his company to handle the insurance for the Alliance on a flat percentage basis. From the beginning it was a choosy arrangement in which the poor risks were not admitted to the Alliance. Those who took the necessary steps to protect themselves against loss by fire received full insurance at reasonable cost.

In 1917, when Jimmy Lynn became the Epperson general manager, the insurance premiums ran somewhere less than a million dollars a year, and the resources of the Lumbermen's Underwriting Alliance were under a million. Today the annual premiums are around six millions, and the resources have grown to more than thirteen millions.

Rapid Progress Under Lynn

A period of rapid growth started immediately after Lynn bought the Epperson business. He attributed it to the talents of people in the organization. These talents were encouraged by his policy of turning people loose to show what they could do, a policy that also involved paying salaries according to demonstrated ability. As summed up by one employee, it was a case of opening the door to individual opportunity.

The prodigious loan made by E. F. Swinney could have been paid back in three or four years. Such were the profits from the stimulated business. When the loan was reduced to manageable size, Lynn chose to expand. The second year he moved into the field of reciprocal insurance for motorcar dealers. They had formed their own Universal Underwriters exchange which had $57,000 of premiums when Lynn took over the management. The exchange now has premiums of around $4,500,000, and covers one-fourth of the factory-authorized dealers in the country. Like the lumber companies, the automobile dealers come into their exchange on a highly selective basis that holds down the total.

The Lynn sideline in citrus fruits started in 1927 with a twenty-acre ranch. He discovered that he couldn't get top management for a ranch of that size, so he expanded to 500 acres.

His oil business started in 1938 on the kind of deal he wouldn't take today. In the middle of a large Illinois oil field a stubborn farmer held out for $50,000 as the price of a lease on 100 acres. The big and experienced operators wouldn't take it. Lynn paid the $50,000 and got a dry hole for a start. The second drilling job produced one of the best wells in the field and he was on his way.

A Philanthropic Gesture for a Beloved City

The only strictly public job accepted by James J. Lynn was service on the park board. It might have been connected in his mind with reverence for the outdoors and life close to nature.

After he had resigned from the board he had an opportunity to sell the tract of land on Sixty-third Street for an outdoor theater. It happened to be near the new Sixty-third Street entrance of Swope Park, so Mr. Lynn telephoned J. V. Lewis, the park superintendent. Lewis had been saddened by the thought of a private business beside the new entrance.

"Well, the only way to make sure the park is protected is to put the land in the park," said Mr. Lynn. "I'm giving it to the city."

A Westerner in *samadhi* (superconsciousness), Jan. 1937, Encinitas. Mr. Lynn said: "The love and joy of God that I feel is without any end. One can never forget it once he has tasted it; it is so great he could never want anything else to take its place."

Paramahansaji and Mr. Lynn, Self-Realization headquarters, Jan. 14, 1933 — one year after their first meeting. "Some people say, 'The Western man cannot meditate.' That is not true," Master declared. "Since Mr. Lynn first received *Kriya Yoga*, I have never seen him when he was not inwardly communing with God."

Words of Paramahansa Yogananda about Mr. Lynn (Rajarsi Janakananda)

(The following is a letter to Mr. Lynn, written by Paramahansa Yogananda in Kansas City, February 27, 1932 — a few weeks after their first meeting.)

The Great Ones choose able, willing devotees on earth to deliver other men from ignorance and suffering. On your human life the immortals have put their invisible hands. God and the Masters could employ miracles to create big temples, but that would not change souls. But when the Great Ones find a man who makes a fragrant altar of his heart, They come there to dwell and to work goodness.

The Great Ones love to establish a temple of Spirit in true devotees like you, that wisdom-hungry men may come there to feast on the divine manna. Rejoice! And I too rejoice that the Spirit has taken the flute of your life to play the divine song of Self-realization and to lure other children back to His home.

Let us set ablaze new altars of Self-realization all over America. Let us help to drive away all darkness in men. Let us leave on this dreamlife our spiritual footprints, that others may follow them to banish misery-making nightmares. Let us speak to all about the divine regions where dark dreams dare not tread, where God's fountains of bliss gush forth in ever-new ways to enthrall us, and where we may satisfy all the beautiful desires and fancies of the human soul.

I send you my deepest love, and my covenant to be your friend forever. When we have crossed the portals of finitude and incarnations, we shall reach the bosom of the Divine Friend and become one with Him.

You are a Hindu yogi of Himalayan hermitages of the past, appearing in this life as an American prince, a Western maharaja-yogi who will light the lamp of Self-realization in many groping hearts.

(Paramahansa Yogananda wrote the following letter to Mr. Lynn; dated October 13, 1933, Indianapolis.)

Most blessed, beloved, little one, I have been so intoxicated with the God in you, and with the remembrance of the pillar of light that we saw enveloping us during the meditation in Chicago, that I did not realize I have been so long in writing you. You have never before been so strongly present in me. (You are always with me now, so I can't miss you.) So vividly have I seen your soul, like a glittering jewel and an ornament in God's omnipresence!

I have been most happy since the Lord sent such a one as you to look after His work with me. I was tired of hollowhearted people who wanted respect from me because of their riches. I shrink from people who expect me to appeal slavishly to them for funds to carry on this work for the world. I and my dear ones here at the Mt. Washington Center would rather go hungry than beg a crumb from anyone who thinks that the anchor of life is not God, but material possessions.

I do not try to write you often, as I see you in God. Just a little while ago a great, infinite tide was tumbling about in my heart, and I saw you swimming steadfastly with me to His shore. You are more fortunate than a million earthly kings, for God has given you self-control and a deep willingness to meditate. He is steadily drawing you unto Him. The most destructive shaft of *maya*-delusion is unwillingness to meditate, and thus to prevent oneself from tuning in with God and guru.

⚌

(The following is a letter to Mr. Lynn, written by Guruji in 1934. By it we understand that in 1934 Master already knew that Mr. Lynn would spend his last years in California, meditating in quietude rather than becoming "entangled with the details of our organization." The last two paragraphs, also, are beautifully prophetic.)

Some day I know God will free you from your business life and then you may come here to meditate on these sacred hills in complete ecstasy with God. When you are thus free, I would not want you to be entangled with the details of our organization. I would want you only to revel in the Infinite. When you get a pension from the Divine Mother to retire from your business life, there will be no more work for you — only thinking, meditating, and talking with Her.

In Plato's story of the two stallions, one stallion was turned heavenward; the other earthward. But you and I both are turned heavenward; both are pulling the chariot of this work to the goal of divine fulfillment. Both of us, directed by the Great Ones, are necessary to draw the vehicle to its goal. That God has given me the privilege to serve is my blessed good fortune. I want nothing; my only desire is that I may establish this work as a divine oasis where aspiring souls may quench their thirst.

Paramahansaji and Mr. Lynn have just risen from meditation (*see page 24*).
The love shining in their eyes as they would gaze at each other was beautiful
to behold. "How outstandingly great, outstandingly gracious, outstandingly
kind he was!" Mr. Lynn said of his guru.

Playing Our Parts in the Cosmic Movie

When your bodily changes do not affect your hoard of acquired spiritual realizations and your love for God, know then that you have become firmly established in Him. At heart renounce everything, and realize that you are just playing a part in the intricate Cosmic Movie, a part that sooner or later must be over. You will then forget it as a dream. Our environment produces the delusion in us of the seeming importance of our present roles and our present tests. Rise above that temporal consciousness. So realize God within that He becomes the only environment, the only ambition, the only influence in your life. You must work just to please Him. Meditate to bring Him on the altar of peace. Bliss is the only altar where God comes. He does not accept any other vibration, any other invitation.

When you and I have fulfilled our mission on earth, we shall be released. Then we shall be free to stay in heaven or to come back here. When we are free we may take trips to earth to load our boats with shipwrecked souls and to bring them safely to the divine shores.

A Vision of Reunion After Death

I write this now, as I see this vision as I sit on my roof[1] under the sunlight, encircled by the Infinite. When you come to me in future, together we shall rejoice exultantly, merging as one in the Eternal Sea.

(*Extracts from a speech by Paramahansaji, January* 3, 1937, *Los Angeles, at a banquet held in his honor to celebrate his return to America after a visit to India in* 1935-6.)

Paramahansaji Often Called the Disciple "Saint Lynn"

It is because of Mr. Lynn's great love for God that I have given him the title of "Saint." In him, and in a number of others in the West, has been fulfilled a prophecy uttered by our great Master, Babaji[2] of India, who said in 1894: "The vibrations of many spiritually seeking souls in the West come floodlike to me. I perceive potential saints in America and Europe, waiting to be awakened."

The love and friendship of St. Lynn, and the affection of many other wonderful souls, have brought me back to this country. I had thought I might not return here. All places are the same to me because

---

[1] See photograph of the roof on page 39.
[2] Mahavatar Babaji, guru of Lahiri Mahasaya (see page 92).

Mr. Lynn on a seagirt rock, Encinitas, 1936. "The love of God is the only Reality," he said. "We must realize this love of God — so great, so joyful, I could not even begin to tell you how great it is!"

they are filled with the omnipresent Spirit. When I close my eyes, I am with my Father; I don't know whether my body is in India or in America. But the love of these friends brought me back here again.

In friendship there is no compulsion. In all other human relationships there is some form of compulsion, but friendship is the natural and spontaneous gift of the heart. St. Lynn and I live in the greatest joy and friendship. What I had expected of him in spiritual development, he has more than fulfilled. He represents the best in American business principles as well as in universal spiritual principles.

In the Encinitas hermitage, St. Lynn and I have been meditating day and night. I have a hard time even to get him to eat or sleep. In this country I have never before known such unity and friendship, such divine communion.

≈

(*Extracts from a talk given by Paramahansaji at an SRF gathering, Los Angeles, California, January* 18, 1940.)

Of all the women I have met in America, I think the one who has found highest favor with God is Sister Gyanamata [1869-1951]. Of all the men I have met here, I think the one who has found highest favor with God is St. Lynn.

St. Lynn, more than most of us, is busy with many large affairs. Still, he and I hardly ever talk business or worldly matters. We meditate together.

Most Men Have Never Explored Soul Possibilities

A businessman of his type is expert in weighing comparative values. By his own efforts he has enabled himself to judge fairly between the worth of mundane joys and the worth of spiritual joys. Most people think that money will bring happiness, but they have no correct standard of comparison. They have never explored the possibilities of soul happiness. All the joys they know about are physical, material, and mental joys. Of the blissful soul-realm they know nothing. If, like St. Lynn, they follow a scientific path, *Kriya Yoga,* that opens up the hitherto unknown route to the soul, all men will someday be able to declare: "Once I knew myself only as a body; now I know myself as Spirit."

Some people say: "The Western man cannot meditate." That is not true. I gave *Kriya Yoga* initiation to St. Lynn shortly after I had met him; and since then I have never seen him when he was not inwardly

On the lotus pool, grounds of SRF Hermitage, Encinitas, 1938. Yoganandaji said of Mr. Lynn: "In him, and in a number of others in the West, has been fulfilled a prophecy uttered by our great Master, Babaji, who said: 'The vibrations of many spiritually seeking souls in the West come floodlike to me. I perceive potential saints in America and Europe, waiting to be awakened.'"

communing with God. It is that most beautiful part of his nature which I enjoy. Whatever the subjects of our conversations, our meetings always end in deep meditation.

St. Lynn Prefers Meditation to Seeing World's Fair in Chicago

I remember, for instance, an occasion in 1933. I went to Chicago to give a lecture at the Parliament of Religions that was a feature of the great World's Fair. St. Lynn left Kansas City at the same time in order to meet me in Chicago. But he came only to meditate with me. While millions of people poured into the city to see the wonders on display, St. Lynn never went near the Fair!

Everyone who takes the spiritual path seriously will find that *Kriya Yoga* will take him as far as he wants to go: to God Himself. The Lord has no favorites. To him who loves God, to him He surrenders. But He cannot be known except through communion. No matter how many good works you do; no matter how much service you render to humanity; no matter how vast your philanthropies — they are not enough. To know God, direct communion through meditation is necessary.

Wooing the Divine First Lady of the Universe

God is like a beautiful, highborn, inaccessible princess. Many men seek her hand in marriage and send her magnificent gifts. But the one who wins her *does more* than the others. By the exercise of long, patient ingenuity he succeeds in meeting her, and, finally, in convincing her of his eternal love.

The case is similar between the truth seeker and God. No outward gestures, however grand, convince the Divine Great Lady that the devotee will die of unrequited love unless he can meet Her. That conviction may be conveyed to Her only face to face. *Kriya Yoga* is a sacred password that opens the doors of the Palace and secures the longed-for audience.

≈

(*The following is a letter written by Paramahansaji to Mr. Lynn; dated May 5, 1940.*)

This letter is written on your birthday to tell you how much India and I appreciate the precious gift of the Father in your birth. You were born for the sake of world upliftment. The good that has passed, by your instrumentality, through the Self-Realization work is appreciated not only by India and by those who know you here but also by the Heavenly Father.

Paramahansa Yogananda and Rajarsi Janakananda in SRF Hermitage garden, Encinitas, California, 1938

I especially appreciate your birthday; for, besides being a gift to the world, you are a personal gift from God to me of the highest, sincerest, and sweetest friendship. And this is my prayer: that in my eyes you stand higher and higher in esteem and love, becoming continuously more spiritually progressive, that I may ever relate the same to my Father — He who has delegated me on earth to usher you in love's chariot to His everlasting kingdom.

May your example be a beacon light of inspiration to spiritual seekers on earth and in the astral world hereafter. May your life be the model after whose ideal pattern devotees of East and West will shape their own lives.

My soul expresses this perception about you, on this, your birthday.

(The following are excerpts from a speech given by Paramahansaji at an SRF gathering in Los Angeles on June 29, 1941.)

I have accepted students in all stages of spiritual development and have tried earnestly to train many of them. Some have failed on the path, but a large number have fulfilled their promise to God. The extraordinarily fast progress toward emancipation shown by a few devotees, like Mr. Lynn, is a source of deep happiness to me. One moon gives more light than countless stars.

Mr. Lynn's Simple Habits and Balanced Life

I know how religiously Mr. Lynn conducts his life. He doesn't drink or smoke. He follows a simple diet of vegetables and fruit juices. He leads a celibate life. He doesn't go to the movies. For recreation he sits on the grass and meditates on the Divine. His whole existence is an exalted one, even though he attends to heavy business duties and is required to travel extensively in connection with his business responsibilities. He has had many temptations thrown in his way, but he has not succumbed to them. He has felt that Joy within which is greater than anything the world can offer. "Lord, Thou art more tempting than any other temptation."

A Westerner Proves the Worth of Yoga

I am proud that in Mr. Lynn a Westerner has stepped forth to show the world the worth in daily life of yoga training. Through him the lives of many, many men will be profoundly changed and turned toward God.

Rajarsi and Paramahansa Yogananda in pulpit of Self-Realization Fellowship Church of All Religions, Hollywood, California, 1942. Whenever Mr. Lynn would arrive in Los Angeles from Kansas City, Paramahansaji would garland the disciple in the Indian fashion.

In a talk at the SRF Church in Hollywood on April 7, 1952, Rajarsi said: "I am going to address you as the children of God, the children of Master, of the God that is in Master. Our guru came out of the East to the West to bring us, by the example of his life and by his spoken and written words, a divine message of conscious union with God. It was the Heavenly Father that chose Paramahansaji, incarnated him, and sent him to America, that he might bring us all closer to Him."

Paramahansa Yogananda and Mr. Lynn, on grounds of SRF Hermitage, Encinitas, California, 1940. Paramahansaji said: "Mr. Lynn and I live in the greatest joy and friendship. What I expected of him in spiritual development, he has more than fulfilled. He represents the best in American business principles as well as in universal spiritual principles."

Mr. Lynn's Words
about Paramahansa Yogananda
and the Self-Realization Path

(In 1937 Mr. Lynn attended an SRF banquet given in Los Angeles, California, to celebrate the return of Paramahansaji from his eighteen-month tour of India and Europe. The following speech by Mr. Lynn was given on January 3, 1937.)

Just five years ago I had the great privilege of meeting Paramahansa Yogananda for the first time. I had always been interested in truth and religion, although I had never accepted any church. My life was business; but my soul was sick and my body was decaying and my mind was disturbed. I was so nervous I couldn't sit still.

An Experience of the Healing Light

After I had met Paramahansaji and had been with him a little while, I became aware that I was sitting very still; I was motionless; I didn't seem to be breathing. I wondered about it and looked up at Paramahansaji. A deep white light appeared, seeming to fill the entire room. I became a part of that wondrous light. Since that time I have been free from nervousness.

I found that I had discovered something real, something immensely valuable to me. I had had to be sure. Not until my experience of the healing light did I realize that I had found entrance into a spiritual realm previously unknown to me.

The beautiful thing in these teachings is that one doesn't have to depend on blind beliefs. He experiences. He *knows* he knows, because he experiences. Ordinarily man is conscious only of his thoughts and of the material world that he can smell, taste, touch, see, and hear. But he is not conscious of the soul deep within him that makes it possible for him to think and to cognize the outer world through his senses. He doesn't know anything about That which is behind the scenes, just behind the thoughts and senses. One should learn to realize the presence

of this Life, the real Life; and attain the union of his own consciousness
with that Life.

Wealth Without Wisdom Cannot Give Joy

Before I met Paramahansaji the thought had not occurred to me
that man could be conscious to a fuller extent than I was at that time.
Yet, having enjoyed the things of the world, I had come to a point of
distress; because, as I said a moment ago, my soul was sick and my body
was not well. Nothing seemed to satisfy me. If you have had an opportunity to observe the rich, those with vast possessions, you have found
that most of them are discontented and unhappy. Wealth without wisdom
cannot give joy. All of us are seeking joy in life; in everything we do
we are seeking happiness.

Self-Realization Path — A Blend of Yoga and Devotion

On the path of Self-realization one becomes alive again. He actually
lives. He feels the divine Life within him. He experiences the union of
his individual soul with the universal Spirit. The Self-realization path
as taught by Paramahansaji is scientific. It is a combination of yoga — a
science that is practiced within one's own being — and devotion to
God. Together, yoga and devotion will bring man to a realization of
his own divinity.

Religion can have but one purpose: knowledge of one's own life
as the omnipresent Life. That attainment is Heaven. From my own
experience I am firmly of this opinion: without making a successful
effort to achieve soul-realization, man cannot win salvation or final
freedom in Spirit.

A Combination Needed of Western and Eastern Treasures

America is rich in material accomplishments. And India is rich in the
wisdom of Spirit. A combination of the two will lead to an ideal
world-civilization.

One who lives in the material world alone, in the consciousness
of materiality, is attached to possessions. Attachment develops slavery.
We become slaves to habits and possessions. It is not possessions that
make us slaves, but ignorance and attachment.

One with material attachments is never free. He has placed his faith
in things that he is bound to lose. Only one possession is lasting: Spirit.
Take the Spirit out of anything and it has no attraction at all. Life is
truly Spirit.

Two things stay with us when the body goes: life and consciousness.
We can get rid of everything except life and consciousness. Those are

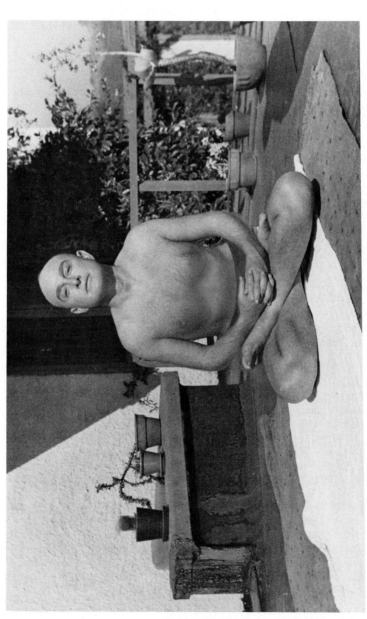

Mr. Lynn in meditation at the Mother Center, 1937. The disciple's slight smile conveys an intimation of the bliss that he habitually enjoyed in God-communion. "A master is not a master of someone else, but of himself," he said. "Even God does not try to master others. He has given us life, consciousness, and free will to live the divine life if we choose."

eternally with us. Self-Realization Fellowship teachings show one how to develop a proper consciousness — an awareness and inner experience of Spirit.

Paramahansaji doesn't ask his students to accept anything as a matter of belief only. "Practice *Kriya Yoga,*" he says, "and discover for yourself the glories of the soul within."

Paramahansaji, Embodiment of Love

A master is like an angel of God. In our beloved Paramahansaji we have one who is the very embodiment of love and unselfishness. He is the possessor of divine joy. His contact goes back to a chain of illumined masters.[1] To the Western mind this statement may sound a little strange, but it is true. The masters are linked, one with another. They have contact with the Spirit, and through their powers that Spirit is transmitted to other men. What a blessing it has been for us that India (a country that many people think of as a land of snake charmers) sent to our shores a master who can help us to achieve God-consciousness.

Those who commune with Spirit know a beauty, a sweetness, that is not experienced in any other way.

How heavenly it is to enjoy the company of a saint! Of all the things that have come to me in life, I treasure more than all else the blessings Paramahansaji has bestowed on me.

The Ancient Hindus Developed a Soul Science

I must admit I was prejudiced at first. Once I was one of those who thought of Hindus as snake charmers. Now I revere India as the land whose saints develop the highest of all sciences — yoga, the techniques for soul-exploration.

(Extracts from a speech delivered by Mr. Lynn, Jan. 8, 1938, Encinitas, California, at the first anniversary celebration of the founding of Self-Realization Fellowship Ashram Center in Encinitas.)

I would rather keep silent than say very much. I would rather feel and realize than talk. But today I would like to tell you a little bit about the blessings that come to one from Self-Realization Fellowship teachings. The first blessing is calmness. We cannot have peace without poise. In 1932, when I first met Paramahansa Yogananda, I was afflicted with extreme nervousness. Since that time one of the greatest joys that

---

[1] See page 92.

The baby is the son of Yoshio Hamada, Japanese gardener at the
SRF Hermitage in Encinitas. The child's name is James Lynn Hamada.

The superintendent at Lynn Farms, Borrego Springs, was a Japanese,
George Shintaku. Imbued with great reverence for his employer, George
would present himself, freshly bathed, every evening at Mr. Lynn's door
for a *darshan* (the blessing that one receives in gazing on a saint).

has come into my life is serenity. Everyone, I now know, can be calm and peaceful.

As a boy I lived in the country. I had some hound dogs whose sense of smell was very keen. Every time they smelled the game they were tracking they would give a yelp. That is how people of the world act — those who live in the senses: they give a yelp whenever they have sensations of pain or pleasure. They have not learned that true life and joy do not depend on sensory experiences. We must find the source of happiness and joy. And that source is God.

The Blessings of Self-Realization Fellowship Teachings

Another great blessing that comes to the SRF devotee is physical and mental health. If our minds are unsettled and uncontrolled, eventually our bodies will be disturbed. We will burn up energy faster than we can receive it. Our minds will be like the inconstant flicker of a candle. In that state we cannot be peaceful or happy or calm. Until we release our minds from a sense of constant strain, we are unable to enjoy true health.

We think our life depends on breath. We believe we have got to be breathing all the time. In a room where the air is not fresh we get sleepy and lose our energy. But an SRF yogi learns how to calm and control the breath. How wonderful it is to be able to sit perfectly still without breath and to live directly on the cosmic energy that is all about us and within us! If that is not a blessing which a man should give his life to find and enjoy, I don't know what anyone could rightly call a blessing!

Consciousness is the one thing that we can never get away from. It is the one thing that is ours and that nobody can deprive us of. It is the gift of our Creator. It is God Himself residing within us.

India has concentrated on understanding the consciousness of man. The right state of consciousness, devotion to God, and following *Kriya Yoga* technique as brought to us from India are a sure way to happiness. In a very short time the teachings of Paramahansa Yogananda can make a greater contribution to our lives — health, happiness, peace of mind, and realization of the fullness of our being — than can all the comforts offered by the developments of material science.

Man is not God, but God is in man. The sooner we realize that He dwells in us the sooner we come to the realization of what our real life is. We have an urge for something higher; we don't know what it is. But it is an urge for happiness and joy — happiness that lies within us. We cannot find it until we discover it within the soul.

MR. LYNN AND GURUJI, CHRISTMAS DAY, 1936

The photograph was taken at a banquet at Self-Realization Fellowship headquarters, Los Angeles. Guruji had just returned from a visit to India. Mr. Lynn is wearing two gifts from his guru: a "Gandhi cap" and a long shawl from Kashmir.

Mr. Lynn said: "I revere India as the land whose saints developed the highest of all sciences — yoga, the techniques for soul-exploration.

"How grateful we should be to a people whose greatest men, down the centuries, have given their lives, have renounced everything else, in order to explore the divine potentialities in man! America is rich in material accomplishments. And India is rich in the wisdom of Spirit. A combination of the two will lead to an ideal world-civilization."

Honor Due India for Her Spiritual Investigations

India, in the person of one of her great masters, Paramahansa Yogananda, has brought to us this priceless knowledge of soul-realization. How grateful we should be to a people whose greatest men, down the centuries, have given their lives, have renounced everything else, in order to explore the divine potentialities in man! What India has given us today in Paramahansaji's teachings is worth more to us than anything we could give to India in exchange. Today the Western man is in dire need of a spiritual technique for developing his soul resources.[1] That technique is *Kriya Yoga,* an ancient science brought to us for the first time by a master from India.

If everything man can possess is outside of him, and if everything that creates impressions on him comes from outside, could he be said to have a true "life" of his own? He must go within to find true life.

"I Have Learned to Live by Inward Joy"

Those of us who are open-minded enough and sincere enough to investigate the truths that Paramahansaji exemplifies are certainly the most blessed people of America. I see that — from my own experience. From following the SRF teachings I have received calmness, peace, joy, wisdom, and all the other blessings of life. No longer does it make much difference whether or not I have anything from the external world; I have learned to live by inward joy. It is the most beautiful thing that life can offer.

After you have reached that state of soul happiness, you can melt yourself into Spirit — a blissful state beyond the finite comprehension. And that joy is the one thing that we are all in search of; it is the one possession that man pursues from life to life. Wherever he goes he will search for that divine happiness. That ever-new Joy is God. It comes by one's own Self-realization. And when a man attains Self-realization he naturally has fellowship with his brothers, because he knows he is one with all.

May I ask that all of you stand as a tribute to our Paramahansa Yogananda? We are paying homage to the great soul that resides in the body sitting here. But he is not confined to a fleshly frame. That is just the state in which we see him with our physical eyes. If our hearts

---

[1] One out of every twelve children born in the United States will spend some time in a mental institution, according to a report published on March 7, 1955, by the Hoover Commission on Government Reorganization. The report states that more than half the hospital beds in the nation are now used by the mentally ill. — *Editor.*

Mr. Lynn on beach at Encinitas, 1937. He said: "In the knowledge and wisdom that Paramahansa Yogananda brings to us we are able to realize, consciously feel, and know unshakably that our soul is one with Spirit. What greater blessing, what greater assurance could one have?"

are receptive we glimpse much more in him than we can see and touch with the senses. If our consciousness is attuned to spiritual truths we perceive in him something that is beyond the power of the senses to detect: the Divine Life.

I appreciate your getting up to pay tribute to this great man, this spiritual teacher who has the wisdom that "surpasseth understanding."

(The following are extracts from a talk given by Mr. Lynn at an SRF gathering in Los Angeles, California, on January 18, 1940.)

The perfect fulfillment we are all seeking will come to us through Self-realization. And what is Self-realization? Consciousness of God — inner perception that your very life is God. That awakening or awareness will come to you when you are able to contact God through the teachings of a true guru. Jesus said, "I do nothing of myself."[1] He gave the credit to God. The man of wisdom claims nothing for himself; he is without ego. He realizes that God is the only One that does anything. His alone is the Power.

In the SRF path we don't give up anything worthwhile. We actually find that for which we have been constantly searching. We will never be content until our deepest search is rewarded. It is through the teachings and blessings of a master, our master, that we may receive that which we seek.

Our Business Duties may be Carried on Harmoniously

If we are at peace within our beings, we can harmoniously carry on our duties even in the business sphere. We can accomplish admirable things in the world without necessarily clashing with others. After our day's work is over we can retire within to be with God again. Eventually, even in the business world, we can perform all our duties with the full consciousness of God's presence. If we are calm and peaceful, come what may — success or seeming failure — we remain even-minded, feeling the certainty that His will is being done.

If we could gain the whole world, and have nothing else but the world, we would not find happiness. Earthly possessions cannot bestow peace and joy. *God can.*

Divine consciousness is That which is the essential part of our being. It is possible to realize That. It is possible to experience It. We don't have to take anyone else's word for it. We may realize ourselves

---

[1] *John* 8:28.

Rajarsi Janakananda at Borrego Springs, Sept. 1954. Of him Paramahansa Yogananda said: "I am proud that in Mr. Lynn a Westerner stepped forth to show the world the worth in daily life of yoga training. Through him the lives of many, many men will be profoundly changed and turned toward God."

MEANING OF NAME, "RAJARSI JANAKANANDA"

Janakananda means "the bliss of Janaka." Janaka was a great king as well as a fully Self-realized master of ancient India.

Rajarsi, literally, "royal rishi," comes from the Sanskrit *raja*, "king" + *rsi* or *rishi*, "great saint." Paramahansaji said: "For you, St. Lynn, I interpret this title as 'king of the saints.'"

as partaking in the life of God Himself. We need not separate ourselves from Him.

After one has experienced the divine consciousness, he enjoys it immeasurably more than he enjoys anything else. *I have found that nothing the world can give me is comparable to the joy of meditation and the consciousness of God's presence.*

We have to make the effort ourselves. But if we allow our will to be led by the wisdom of a master whose will is in tune with God's, the master then seeks to guide our will in such a way that we travel swiftly on the road back to divinity. The chief difference between a worldly man and a saint is that the wise man has attuned his will to the Divine Will.

We say that God is omnipresent. The word omnipresent has only a vague meaning for most people. Could it be otherwise when they must imagine it only? Imagination cannot convey the sense of omnipresence; only experience can do that. True spiritual experience is realization of the very presence within us of the Infinite God.

We don't have to feel that the consciousness of Jesus was different from that of any God-illumined master of India. The real master, whether in India or in this country or anywhere else, is he who is one with God. He has united his soul with Him. The power he manifests is simply the divine current flowing through him.

All Illumined Men Live in the Same Divine Consciousness

After soul-realization we may read all scriptures understandingly. Otherwise we don't get the true significance of words of the prophets. You will find that all scriptures confirm the teachings of every great master. The Bibles of the world confirm everything that Self-Realization Fellowship undertakes to teach us. There is no essential difference.

It is within the power of every one of us to attain true wisdom. We have to make the effort. It is up to us. We must meditate to attain deep faith. After we have received the first contact of God, we should then seek to develop the contact into a greater and greater consciousness. That is what Jesus asked everyone to do. He wanted them to receive his omnipresent consciousness. And that is what Paramahansaji teaches. He brings us God and all he asks is that we receive.

May you tune your will to God's will and make the effort to attain Self-realization! When you have found the teachings that can bring you to God, accept them. Know your Heavenly Father and enjoy His glory.

Paramahansaji and Mr. Lynn playing with a toy airplane, a Christmas gift from guru to disciple, on a porch at the hermitage, Encinitas, 1947.

Mr. Lynn, 1947. He was close to Nature; healthful sun baths in the privacy of the hermitage grounds were a daily feature of his visits to Encinitas. His was truly a balanced life — the ideal of the sages. He was successful in the business world and on the spiritual path. He never neglected his body; for its sake he formed every good habit of diet, outdoor living, and physical exercise as taught by Paramahansaji.

(*Mr. Lynn made the following speech on February 20, 1948. The occasion was the annual Flower Show in Encinitas, California, where some of the finest perfume-essence flowers in America are grown. The SRF gardens in Encinitas were represented at the Show with a display of cyclamens, caladiums, hydrangeas, and cinerarias. Later in the day Mr. Lynn spoke again at the unveiling of three towers, erected along the main thoroughfare to mark the grounds of the Encinitas Ashram Center.*)

Most people go through life wondering what it is all about. They know many things, but little about themselves. All human beings are created under divine law; but if they are ignorant of the divine laws, they know little if anything about how life should be lived. We assume at times to understand a great deal. When we think we know a lot, that is the time that each of us had better ask himself: "Do I know anything about my real Self?"

Man in his Human Aspect Cannot Find Happiness

We go through life expecting to get our pleasures from the outward world, from the money we make, from the things we build up — but all of these perish. Therefore, in the innermost depths of our hearts, we are dissatisfied. We find at times that, after all, we are not so big. We don't amount to so much. When we take a true inventory of ourselves, free from vanity, we find that we are a very insignificant particle of life.

And so I am grateful that in my progress through life I found Paramahansa Yogananda. When I met him I was a man very busy with many affairs. I thought I had accumulated some of the worthwhile things of life; yet I was not happy. I had found that everything I obtained lost its value. When I had obtained it, its attraction disappeared. I could not be happy, and yet I went along as best I could. I never thought that someday I would find a great teacher who would give me an understanding of my Self.

The Blessings I Have Found through Paramahansaji

One of the blessings I have received in my friendship with Paramahansa Yogananda has been permanent relief from a state of nervousness, a state of strain, an inward state of uncertainty. I have gained calmness, peace, joy, and a sense of security that cannot come to anyone until he has found the true security of the soul. Paramahansaji has brought me this understanding, this blessing of knowledge of the law of man's real being.

As I walked through the flower show today I thought of the flowers as one of the greatest creations of God. In them we find beauty,

A GREAT YOGI OF THE EAST AND A GREAT YOGI OF THE WEST—MASTERS OF THEMSELVES

Yogananda and James J. Lynn in yoga posture on the private grounds of SRF Hermitage, Encinitas, California, 1950. "The balanced life of Mr. Lynn may serve as an inspiration for all men," the great guru said. Conscientiously discharging the duties of his worldly life, Mr. Lynn yet found time daily for deep meditation on God. The successful businessman became an illumined *Kriya Yogi*.

color, and perfume. But the loveliness of the soul is greater than the beauty of the flower. Yet the soul cannot be known in its vast and glorious nature, cannot express itself in man's daily life, so long as he remains in ignorance of himself.

Man is an intelligent being, a wonderful being; but he must be conscious of himself, of his true nature. When our consciousness is limited to the senses we are not aware of our real being.

Yoga is the Science of the Soul

Yoga is the science by which one unites his soul with Spirit. A yogi is one who employs definite meditation techniques in order to realize his true nature of soul, united forever with the Absolute Spirit, or God. Without such knowledge of the soul, we are not capable of understanding the laws under which God has created us.

In the knowledge and wisdom that Paramahansa Yogananda brings to us we are able to attain a true consciousness of the meaning of our own life. We are able to realize, consciously feel, and know unshakably that our soul is one with Spirit. What greater blessing, what greater assurance could one have?

∙≈∙

(After the passing of Paramahansa Yogananda on March 7, 1952, Mr. Lynn assumed the presidency of SRF-YSS and was thereafter called "Rajarsi Janakananda," the name Guruji had chosen for him. Rajarsi gave the following talk at India Hall, Hollywood, California, on April 7, 1952. The occasion was a banquet, attended by 250 Self-Realization students, celebrating the first anniversary of India Hall. The structure was designed by the guru and built in 1951 by SRF members.)

I am going to address you as the children of God, the children of Master, of the God that is in Master. Our guru came out of the East to the West to bring us, by the example of his life and by his spoken and written words, a divine message of conscious union with God. It was the Heavenly Father who chose Master, incarnated him, and sent him to America, that he might bring us all closer to Him.

Who is a Master?

A master is not a master of somebody else; he is the master of himself. That is the truth we should recognize. We should be masters of ourselves. Even God does not try to master others. He has given us life, consciousness, and free will to live the divine life if we choose. We cannot live in peace or perfection without a sense of our oneness with God.

All Masters Speak the Same Truth

The Christian scriptures give us the same teachings that Master brought to us. The words of all true Sons reveal the One Father.

For those of us who will make the effort, there is still the same opportunity to receive from Master the same consciousness, the same love that was here when he was present with us in the body. Since his passing our awareness of him has increased many times. We should not feel that there has been any loss. I have found the feeling, the realization, the power of his cosmic consciousness to be so great as to be overwhelming.

We are still able to be in communion with Master in spirit; he is with us and is manifesting Life. Do you think that God would send him and then completely withdraw him from us? Surely the Lord does not work that way.[1] Master's coming here was the work of God, for he was chosen by Him to spread the yoga message in the West.

Paramahansaji the Guru of this Path

Master is our guru. There will be no other guru. Is there another preceptor? He will continue as always to be our preceptor.

(Rajarsi presided at the 1952 Convocation, which marked the 32nd anniversary of Self-Realization Fellowship in America. On July 26th, at the Mt. Washington headquarters in Los Angeles, California, Rajarsi gave Kriya Yoga initiation to 400 members. Extracts from his speech at the Convocation on July 27, 1952, are given below.)

My subject is the soul. You may think of the soul as a vague "something." But do you feel it? Do you realize it? Can you be That and not an ego? Can you be That and not a mind? Can you be beyond mind? These questions cannot be answered truly except by those who have discovered by meditation the existence of the soul within.

The soul is a reflection of Spirit. The Absolute God the Father is beyond all creation; we are His myriad reflections in creation. Because

---

[1] "And I will pray the Father, and he shall give you another Comforter [*Aum*], that he may abide with you forever, even the Spirit of truth .... I will not leave you comfortless: I will come to you. Yet a little while, and the world seeth me no more; but ye see me: because I live, ye shall live also. At that day ye shall know that I am in my Father, and ye in me, and I in you." — *John* 14:16-20.

God is a reflection of Himself in each one of us, we can be many, yet all one Father, one Life. And if indeed we are reflections of God, we cannot be only mortal beings. We must be immortal.

But each of us has the power to act as a mortal being or as a god, because God gave us the free choice. When we do our will and not His will, when we act as mortals rather than as His divine children, we violate our own being. And then we must naturally suffer the sad consequences.

What every soul really wants is simply to become one with Spirit. We yearn to be that Life, that Joy, that Love which Master brings to us. Even when I say anything about that Life I feel the presence of Master. He is here! It is impossible for me to speak without feeling this joy of Master's presence. He is not a body; he is not a mind. He is Spirit. He is Life.

I don't care to talk much. I enjoy being this Life, this Spirit, this reflection of God that Master brings to us. He is right here. Master is this joy that I feel. Master brings us this joy, this great power of Spirit. That love of Master's — that love surpassing human understanding — is the love of God. That love is ours. That love is Spirit.

Follow the Plan that Master Taught

You should follow the techniques, the suggestions, the plan, the way that Master brought and gave to you to take you away from the ego, to relieve you from the consciousness of the burdensome body and from the restless mind; to take you into Spirit, into God. Be one with That.

The greatest sin is ignorance — ignorance of the Divine. But you may discover for yourself this joy, this love of Master's, of Spirit. No love was ever so great, so joyful; and he is pouring this love into you. Receive it! You must learn his way, and develop your insight. Know the Power that Master is manifesting. It is real. It is not a matter of imagination or of mere intellectual speculation. It is the eternal foundation of your true being. You must know it. Master brings you the way. When you receive him you will lift yourself into the light, the grace, the wisdom of God.

❧

The following was Rajarsi's Christmas message in 1952 to all members of Self-Realization Fellowship/Yogoda Satsanga Society of India.)

With deep joy in my heart I extend greetings to you at this blessed Christmas season. Seldom before have men so needed to experience the

Paramahansa Yogananda's hands are uplifted in blessing on his beloved disciple, on whom he had just bestowed *sannyas*, and the monastic name of Rajarsi Janakananda; SRF-YSS international headquarters, Los Angeles, August 25, 1951.

true meaning of Christmas — consciously to receive in their hearts the omnipresent love, the joy, the peace of the Christ Consciousness that we celebrate in the coming of Jesus.

Through the blessings of the Masters and our guru Paramahansa Yogananda, and through their Self-Realization Fellowship teachings, my eyes have been opened to the inner spiritual beauty of this season; my heart has been filled with the great love of the omnipresent Christ.

It is my humble wish to share with you this divine love and joy. In our hearts and minds let us gather around the Christmas tree of the world and pray with Jesus Christ and our Gurus that their message of peace, forgiveness, and love to all mankind fall on receptive ears. May all peoples awaken to the light of truth and understanding! Let every heart sing with the angelic chorus, "Glory to God in the highest, and on earth peace, good will toward men."

(The following message from Rajarsi was read to Self-Realization Fellowship center leaders at the Convocation in Los Angeles, August, 1953.)

To you, the center leaders, I am deeply grateful for the wonderful ways in which you are holding aloft the torch of Self-Realization that was first set alight in this land by our incomparable guru Paramahansa Yogananda.

High Responsibilities of Center Leaders

Our center leaders are entrusted with a very special privilege and divine responsibility. All of you, I know, are striving to express in your daily lives the perfect conduct and high ideals that our beloved Master taught by precept and by lifelong example. Let your light so shine before worldly men that they will be inspired to emulate you and thus to regenerate their own lives through *Kriya Yoga.*

To serve as center leaders for the pioneering spiritual movement of Self-Realization Fellowship is not always easy, but the reward is great. God bless you all! I will close with a quotation from our ever-living guru Paramahansaji. On March 6, 1952 — one day before that of his final *samadhi* — he addressed a group of Self-Realization residents and teachers at Mt. Washington. He told them:

"If other men and women fool away their time, *you* be lost in God. You will go ahead. *Prepare yourself. This work will spread all over the world.* Love people with divine love, and be only with those that love

Mr. Lynn in *samadhi* (superconsciousness), summer of 1936. The site of two meditation caves facing the Pacific Ocean was being dug on the grounds of the newly built SRF Hermitage, Encinitas, California.

"No longer does it make much difference whether or not I have anything from the external world," Mr. Lynn said. "I have learned to live by inward joy. It is the most beautiful thing that life can offer."

the Lord. Let your example be the way to change others' lives. Reform yourself and you will reform thousands. Egotism is the hardest thing to overcome. Don't think of yourself. When people say good things about you, give the credit to God. Love Him; cry for Him. What does anything else matter, so long as you find Him? Throw yourself into God, be filled with His love and joy."

(At the garden party on Mt. Washington Estates, Self-Realization headquarters, that concluded the 1953 Convocation, Rajarsi addressed the students. The following is an excerpt from his speech.)

All that I have to give to you is the spirit of Master and of God. I have nothing more to say, nothing more to do except to carry out the wishes that Master had for this great movement. And what he is doing for you these days is not of me. I myself am only this "little one" that he spoke of; and I shall never be more than a little one because it will always be Master, Paramahansaji, who is my life and my blessing to you all.

(Rajarsi was the host at a dinner on Thanksgiving Day, 1953, at the hermitage in Encinitas, California. About fifty SRF devotees attended. The following are excerpts from his speech on that occasion.)

Understand that God is the Only Reality

It is a great blessing, through Master's grace, to have realized myself to be not merely a body but an immortal soul. And someday that will be your own blessing: when you do not identify your Self with the body but know your true nature of Spirit. When you melt into God you will understand that He is the only Reality.

Master is here, just behind the darkness of our closed eyes. Receive the blessing that he gives you even now, and melt with him into the ocean of God's joy. Master wants us to be happy, and he is always with us. Tune in with him and you will never be without the bliss, the love, the peace of God.

(An all-day meditation by devotees on December 23rd is a sacred Christmastime custom established by Paramahansaji. On the morning of December 23, 1953, Rajarsi meditated in Encinitas, California, with the renunciant men disciples; then traveled to Los Angeles to meditate in

Mr. Lynn in *samadhi* (superconsciousness), on the private beach of SRF Hermitage, Encinitas, California, January 1937. "I have found," he said, "that nothing the world can give me is comparable to the joy of meditation and the consciousness of God's presence."

the afternoon with the renunciant women disciples. On December 25, 1953, he presided at a banquet at the Mt. Washington headquarters. The following are excerpts from his speech on Christmas night.)

One does not realize how much he changes as he proceeds along the spiritual path. After I met Master in 1932 I felt changed a great deal; but when he would say to me, "I am in you, and you are in me," I did not quite know what he meant. But now I feel the presence of Master within and around me.

The Love of God — So Great, So Joyful!

The love of God is the only Reality. We must realize this love of God — so great, so joyful, I could not even begin to tell you how great it is! People in the world think, "I do this, I enjoy that." Yet whatever they are doing and enjoying inevitably comes to an end. But the love and joy of God that I feel is without any end. One can never forget it once he has tasted it; it is so great he could never want anything else to take its place. What we all really want is the love of God. And you will have it when you attain deeper realization.

The Great Ones come to bring people back to God. Jesus came to bring realization to all men. And similarly Master came to save us, to bring us back to God. What a blessing many of us possess, to have known Master in this country! But the physical form means little; it is the soul that matters. Master is here now in an even greater way than he was when in the body. It is our joy, our grace, that we can receive his divine vibrations through following the teachings of Self-Realization Fellowship.

≈

(*Meditation services are held annually in all Self-Realization Fellowship temples, ashrams, and centers on January 5th to commemorate Paramahansaji's birthday. Rajarsi spent January 5, 1954, in seclusion at his retreat in Borrego Springs, California. Later he recounted to other disciples of Gurudeva the following sublime experience.*)

A Sacred Experience with Master in the Other World

I awoke around two or three o'clock in the morning on January 5th, and saw Lahiri Mahasaya in the greatest blaze of light in which he has ever manifested to me. Then, one by one, Sri Yukteswar, Babaji,[1] and Master appeared. Master lifted me out of the body and we floated together over many gatherings of people. Master blessed each group as we floated over it. We were not walking, but floating overhead. It seemed as though Master wanted all the people to know that I was with him.

---

[1] See page 92.

I was with Master a long time, from two or three o'clock until nine o'clock — the longest I have ever been with him in this way.

Master is very busy there, just as busy as he was when he lived here — helping the people in those other spheres, teaching them the way of salvation and how to achieve their own Self-realization.

⋙

(The 1954 Convocation, held in August in Los Angeles, marked the 34th anniversary of Self-Realization Fellowship in America. The 400 students who attended the Convocation came from twenty-two states of America and from nine foreign countries. On this occasion the following message from Rajarsi was read.)

The purpose of these Convocations is to bring sincere seekers of truth together for what our guru, Paramahansa Yogananda, called "fellowship with God through Self-realization." This, Master said, is the true significance of the name Self-Realization Fellowship. To followers of this path, therefore, "fellowship" means more than the harmonious feeling engendered when men of like mind gather together to discuss ideas and ideals. To Self-Realization members "fellowship" signifies the blissful sense of universal oneness that comes with the recognition, through meditation, of the individual soul's kinship with the Father and Friend of all.

How True Brotherhood may be Attained

Divine fellowship is necessary before men can know true brotherhood and its natural sequel — peace on earth. The blessed Master was sent to this world to help mankind to understand how to live in fellowship with God and thereby in human brotherhood and true happiness.

You have only to follow the way that Master has shown, with steadfast zeal and devotion, and you will find God. You will realize then, as I do now, that Master is here at this very moment, with you, and with me. Attune yourself that you may know in your soul that Master is here. When Master comes to you, you will realize that nothing exists for you except the love of God; that nothing else is so important to you as His love. Master has melted my soul with his into God. Receive his blessing! Perceive the light of God, and, in it, Master's greatness.

⋙

(The following are a few words of welcome from Rajarsi to Self-Realization students at a Convocation in August 1954, Los Angeles.)

Master through me welcomes you to the 1954 SRF Convocation. This two-in-oneness is not just an idea or an expression of mine; through Master's grace my soul has melted into his, and we are one in God.

Master expresses himself through the humble instrument of this body and mind. But Master would never say that any credit belonged to him — he acknowledged only God as the Doer. God is working through Master, through the Great Ones, that all of us may enjoy, by right action and right meditation, oneness with Him; that we may melt, even as the Masters have done, into the bliss of Spirit.

Remember, as you attend the convocation classes and join in the other spiritual activities that have been planned for you, that Master is here. He is just behind the darkness of closed eyes when we sit to meditate. He is watching and waiting for us as we put forth that steadfast, daily, ever-deepening effort in meditation that makes it possible for him to lift us up to God. He wants us to be happy in the knowledge that he is always here with us. Discovering this, in deepest meditation, we will discover also the joy, the peace, the love of God.

Rajarsi (*center, in front of tree*) presiding over the Christmas Day banquet for monks and nuns of the Self-Realization Order, 1953, Mt. Washington international headquarters, Los Angeles

MR. LYNN'S LAST HOME, BORREGO SPRINGS, CALIFORNIA

Mr. Lynn was born on a farm and died on a farm. His birth took place in a one-room log cabin; his death occurred in a spacious well-appointed home on a 668-acre estate, "Lynn Farms." He often reflected on life's contrasts: an expression of the inexorable law of relativity that governs the phenomenal world. "God is the only Immutable," he said, "the only Security."

———————— ✢✕✢ ————————

RAJARSI OFFICIATED AT GURUJI'S FUNERAL

Rajarsi conducted the last rites for Paramahansa Yogananda at the headquarters on March 11, 1952. At the start of the services a rainbow appeared in the skies. In a beautiful speech at the bier, Rajarsi said: "Master gave us his love as father, mother, and friend. His whole life, his whole expression, his whole satisfaction was in the giving of that great love. How outstandingly great, outstandingly gracious, outstandingly kind he was!"

The Ambassador of India, Mr. Binay Ranjan Sen, spoke at the funeral. His eulogy of Yogananda ended with the words: "Death has no victory in him."

A Miracle at Forest Lawn

The Ambassador's closing words were singularly prophetic. For weeks after Yogananda's death his unchanged face shone with the divine luster of incorruptibility. Manifesting a phenomenal state of immutability, his body emanated no odor of decay. In death, as in life, the great yogi demonstrated the power of Spirit over matter. (The full testimony by Mr. Harry T. Rowe, mortuary director at Forest Lawn Memorial-Park, appears in the booklet, *Paramahansa Yogananda: In Memoriam.*)

Mr. Lynn sampling one of the grapefruits from his 500-acre orchard in the Rio Grande Valley of Texas, 1947. Of him Paramahansa Yogananda said: "His whole existence is an exalted one, even though he attends to heavy business duties and is required to travel extensively in connection with his business responsibilities. He has had many temptations thrown in his way, but he has not succumbed to them. He has felt that Joy within which is greater than anything the world can offer. 'Lord, Thou art more tempting than any other temptation.'"

Press Comments about Mr. Lynn

(*The following appeared on the editorial page of the* Kansas City Times, *Kansas City, Missouri, February* 22, 1955.)

"The success story of James J. Lynn is a fabulous one that has been told and told again. Its beginning was in a tremendous natural ability and in a brilliancy for figures that removed a boy from a cotton farm and placed him on the high levels of big business. Its end found a man searching for something beyond financial success.

"That would seem entirely natural in considering the complex character of a man like James Lynn. He absorbed a belated education while working full time and was admitted to the bar at the age of 21. Three years later he was a certified public accountant. At 24 he was general manager of the U. S. Epperson Underwriting Company, and before he was 30 was the owner (along with a huge debt). Within a few years he had expanded into a half-dozen fields.

"His love of Nature and the fact that he reached a summit of material success at an early age must have contributed to his sincere interest of later years in religious mysticism. His death Sunday in California ends one of Kansas City's most remarkable stories of individual brilliance and achievement."

≈

(*The following appeared in the* Kansas City Star, *Kansas City, Missouri, February* 27, 1955. *The author is James S. Jackson, feature writer for the* Star.)

"James J. Lynn was a very fine gentleman indeed — considerate, friendly, modest in demeanor....

"It was 'Jimmy' Lynn downtown, although few were closely acquainted with this unusual man. He was of youthful, alert appearance, springy of step and bareheaded, ruddy of complexion and with thinning hair; a man with a quick smile. He wore an open shirt, without necktie. That was the Jimmy Lynn Kansas City knew. Citizens were surprised to find that he of the springy step was already a highly successful business man.

"Jimmy Lynn was one of the richer men in Kansas City. The fortune made through insurance underwriting was multiplied by lucky turns in the oil fields of Texas. He was easily the largest stockholder in the Union National Bank.

"Lynn's IQ Would Have Rung the Bell for Genius"

"He didn't appear to be a millionaire, but mentally he was lightning quick in perception and magic with figures. Mathematicswise, Lynn's IQ would have rung the bell for genius. We all know men who are marvels with figures, but no great shucks in business decisions. Lynn was also a man of sound business judgment. And he was extremely lucky. One needs a lucky touch to make millions in Texas oil from a Kansas City base....

"Before he was thirty, Jimmy Lynn headed the Epperson insurance underwriting concerns. It was not luck but the Lynn personality and capabilities that had attracted the attention of U. S. Epperson.

"Lynn himself said his success story was not one that could be duplicated today. Timing was a factor. Ahead of present-day tax laws he was able to buy a large, highly profitable business and to pay for it out of profits. But the deal had called for a sizable equity down-payment. A friend advanced the amount in cash.

A Huge Loan Secured Only by Lynn's Character

"The friend at the needful moment was the late E. F. Swinney of the First National Bank. The borrowing could not qualify as a bank loan. Swinney, watchful of a dollar though he was, advanced the money out of his own pocket. He, too, was paid out of earnings from the expanding business.

"Probably no other single incident in his career afforded Ed Swinney the satisfaction he got from his brief backing of Jimmy Lynn. Swinney, who held solvency to be a major virtue, often recounted that all payments from Lynn came ahead of schedule. He once remarked to this reporter that Lynn, the young man to whom he had lent helpful dollars, had passed him in wealth by two or three times. That was quite a few years ago, too. Swinney, incidentally, left an estate of three million dollars.

"Jimmy Lynn was an odd combination of the competent businessman and the philosopher who stressed closeness to universal forces. He felt he improved the quality of business letters by removing his shoes — inhibitors of foot respiration. The staff respected the keen mental alertness of the barefoot boss.

"Lynn assembled a large estate between Sixty-third Street and Meyer Boulevard. Here he developed in the 20's a private nine-hole

Rajarsi spent as much time as possible in the sunshine and fresh air. Here at the Encinitas hermitage in 1947 he performs a handstand with easy grace. A Kansas City reporter, describing Mr. Lynn's daily outdoor program, wrote:

"Clad only in a loincloth, the astute businessman rolled through exercises on the dewy lawn or lay prone for long periods to draw within himself forces from the good earth.... He was happy for the ample privacy that attended the calisthenics. He could romp like a boy."

golf course. And there in the first hours of the young sun he brought himself close to Nature.

"Clad only in a loincloth, the astute businessman rolled through exercises on the dewy lawn, or lay prone for long periods to draw within himself forces from the good earth. These first hours of the day were important to Lynn, so he habitually had late hours for his office. Once at the office his quick perceptions soon had him abreast of the day.

"This daybreak rendezvous with the rising sun was something Lynn was quite ready to discuss. Of course, he was happy for the ample privacy that attended the calisthenics. He could romp like a boy....

Arranges Golf Course to Please his Older Friends

"Banker Swinney delighted in the short golf course. In fact, when the aging banker had to forego golf, the course was abandoned. Lynn sensed the pleasure his older friends took in their relatively low scores. In most standard golf courses every change introduces fresh hazards, but in the Lynn course every change eased existing difficulties.

"It had been Mr. Swinney's ambition to shoot a 75 on his seventy-fifth birthday, the occasion of a noteworthy party[1] on the Lynn estate in 1932. He did come in with a 76, quite happy and willing to overlook some concessions."

---

[1]The party was attended by about seventy-five guests, among them Judge Kenesaw Mountain Landis, the late commissioner of baseball; Mr. Mellville Taylor, at that time president of the First National Bank of Chicago; and the late Bishop Thomas F. Lillis.

Rajarsi in meditation, Encinitas, August 1953

Messages from Friends and SRF Centers

EMBASSY OF INDIA, WASHINGTON, D. C.: "Mr. G. L. Mehta, the Ambassador of India, regrets to learn the sad news of the death of Mr. James J. Lynn of the Self-Realization Fellowship, and wishes to convey his sincere condolences."

CONSULATE GENERAL OF INDIA, SAN FRANCISCO, CALIFORNIA. Mr. S. K. Banerji, Consul General of India, wrote: "I am grieved to hear that the president of the Fellowship, Rajarsi Janakananda, died. Though I did not have the opportunity of knowing him, I have heard a great deal about him, and would like to convey my condolences to the Fellowship."

DUCI DE KEREKJARTO, concert violinist: "The passing of our beloved Rajarsi is a great loss to all of us. Because he had God's love, he was a man of divine hope. He was at peace with himself and with others. I shall forever honor him for his reassuring voice: that of a good instructor, a faithful servant to the Master Yogananda."

SRF CENTER, MONTREAL, CANADA: "We are indeed sad that Rajarsi is no longer with us; but how wonderful that he is with Master!"

SRF CENTERS IN SWITZERLAND. Mrs. Helen Erba-Tissot wrote: "We must learn to say 'God alone,' and to meditate deeply enough to know what God through Master wishes from each of us. Rajarsi is surely with our beloved Master, and happy. We will go our way courageously, our minds firmly fixed on God."

MRS. G. J. WATUMULL, Watumull Foundation, Honolulu: "Although we did not know Mr. Lynn so well as we knew Paramahansa Yogananda, still we were very fond of Mr. Lynn and admired him tremendously. We all know that he has gone on to a larger and better life."

DR. WLADIMIR LINDENBERG, BERLIN, GERMANY. Dr. Lindenberg, director of a hospital for war-injured veterans in Berlin, wrote: "The news of our dear Rajarsi's *mahasamadhi* reached me today. After Paramahansaji's passing, Rajarsi was the father of Self-Realization Fellowship. I consider Rajarsi to have been a true representative of Paramahansaji, my beloved Guru. Now that Rajarsi is free from the bonds of the body, he will be able to wield a greater spiritual influence than ever before. God bless him, and you all, in the holy work. We will live in His joy, and love one another in the same joy."

SRF CENTER, LONDON, ENGLAND. Mrs. Gertrude White wrote: "It must have been Rajarsi's desire, if indeed he had one at all, to join Master. It is natural for us to miss the physical presence of loved ones; but what a wonderful thought it is that, if only we will work with them, the great loving Masters will guide us also, as they have guided Rajarsi, from body-identification to soul-identification. Through the teachings of Paramahansaji, all our doubts have been removed. Our members had a long meditation on Thursday and Master seemed very close to us."

SRF CENTER, CALABAR, WEST AFRICA: "We held commemorative services on February 23rd and 25th. Lamenting Rajarsi's death, the whole center sends its heartfelt sympathy to Headquarters, praying that all be undiscouraged in carrying on the teachings of the Masters."

SRF MEDITATION GROUP, AUCKLAND, NEW ZEALAND. Mr. Reginald Howan wrote: "We who are so remotely placed in New Zealand have had little opportunity to know our late president and leader. In *Self-Realization Magazine,* however, we have observed his noble presence in pictures, and have read his inspired messages. The humble and unassuming manner in which he quietly took over the leadership on the passing of Paramahansa Yogananda spoke more than words to us of a remarkable personality. To follow immediately in the footsteps of such a Master was a great task for any man; the manner of Rajarsi's accomplishment endeared him to every discerning fellow-devotee on the path of Light.

"We salute Rajarsi Janakananda, who has joined the Great Ones beyond: Jesus, the Master of Galilee; Lahiri Mahasaya; Sri Yukteswar; the beloved Yogananda — that divine line of succession, of elder brethren. We are not separated from them, but rather are growing closer in our fuller realization of the Spirit whose love and power they manifested; a oneness that makes this Self-Realization Fellowship of ours a living power to do good, to destroy evil, and to assist mankind in reestablishing its rightful divine heritage."

(LEFT) Rajarsi Janakananda, Borrego Springs, California, Jan. 13, 1954. (RIGHT) The bedroom in which Rajarsi's death occurred in his home at Lynn Farms, Borrego Springs. In the niche above are pictures of Christ (*center*), of Lahiri Mahasaya and Mahavatar Babaji (*top*), and of Paramahansa Yogananda and Swami Sri Yukteswar (*bottom*).

Mr. Lynn said: "It is within the power of every one of us to attain true wisdom. We have to make the effort. It is up to us. We must meditate to attain deep faith. After we have received the first contact of God, we should then seek to develop the contact into a greater and greater consciousness.

"Paramahansaji doesn't ask his students to accept anything as a matter of belief only. 'Practice *Kriya Yoga*,' he says, 'and discover for yourself the glories of the soul within.'"

A Letter from Mexico City

BY YOGACHARYA J. M. CUARON

Leader of SRF Centers in Mexico Until His Passing in 1967

In the past few years Rajarsi was extremely kind and considerate toward me. During the September week in 1951 that I spent in Encinitas, he and I used to meditate in Master's study every night from eight p.m. until midnight. Many times he told me: "Master is right here with us, and is very much pleased."

One night Rajarsi remarked that he did not have any personal desires, that the only desires he had were Master's desires. "As our guru had wished to visit Mexico again," he said, "now I hope to be able to arrange to visit Mexico." Though that wish was not fulfilled, I am happy that Rajarsi harbored it.

The Spirit of the Guru Dwelt in Rajarsi

Last year, too, when I visited Encinitas, Rajarsi called me three times to his apartment to meditate with him and to give me his blessings. On these occasions he would pat my hand and head in the same way that Master used to do, with the same gestures and expressions. I hardly knew whether it were Rajarsi or Master sitting before me.

On February 22, 1955, our members in Mexico City held a meeting dedicated to Rajarsi's memory. Our meditation was long and deep, and many of us felt his holy presence amongst us.

On March 8th we held commemorative services for the *mahasamadhis* of Paramahansaji and his guru Sri Yukteswarji. A brief talk on their sacred lives was followed by an hour of meditation. The meeting was solemn and beautiful. Each student had brought flowers; the room was fragrant with the odors of flowers and incense. The attendance was large, and included two students from our Armenia SRF Center in the republic of Colombia in South America.

Before the meeting started I requested the students to leave the room quietly after the meditation was over, without speaking one to another, in order that all might carry with them the high spiritual vibrations of the meeting.

The meditation period ended with a playing of a recording of Master's voice, made at the dedication services on August 20, 1950, of the SRF Lake Shrine in Pacific Palisades. His closing words were: "Until we meet again. Peace, Om, Christ. I bow to you all."

73

Yogoda Math, SRF-YSS headquarters in Dakshineswar, India, held services for Rajarsi Janakananda on Feb. 23rd, the same date that funeral services for him were held in Los Angeles. The altar above displays pictures, lovingly garlanded, of Yoganandaji and Rajarsi.

Services at Yogoda Math, India, March 7th. Two photographs of Rajarsi (*bottom*) flank Paramahansaji's picture on memorial altar.

Services for Rajarsi in India

In 1917 Paramahansa Yogananda founded Yogoda Satsanga Society of India. In 1920 he established his international headquarters in America, translating the name in the West as Self-Realization Fellowship.

In India the suffix "ji" is added to names as a mark of respect.

YOGODA MATH, DAKSHINESWAR, WEST BENGAL, YSS headquarters in India. On February 28th Sri Prabhas Chandra Ghosh, vice-president of the Society, sent to the Los Angeles international headquarters the following cable:

"India shares with the rest of the Self-Realization Fellowship world the deepest sorrow at the passing of our beloved president, Rajarsi Janakanandaji. We realize he has been called to the side of Master and that both, from above, will continue to guide us. Members here held memorial services for Rajarsiji on February 23rd to coincide with the time of his funeral in Los Angeles. All members observed a mourning period of fasting and prayer. On Sunday, February 27th, our members gathered again for a memorial service."

Yogoda Math sent a printed card to all YSS members in India, inviting them to attend, on March 7th in Dakshineswar, a joint memorial service for Rajarsiji and Paramahansa Yoganandaji. On that date a large gathering took part in the program of the all-day meeting. Readings from the *Bhagavad-Gita* and the Bible started at eight a.m. and were followed by periods of meditation, prayer, and devotional chanting; by practice of *Hong-Sau* and *Kriya Yoga;* and by a period of Yogoda rejuvenation exercises as taught by Paramahansaji. From four to five p.m.

75

the audience heard readings from Master's books — *Autobiography of a Yogi, Whispers from Eternity,* and *The Master Said.*

Letter From Yogoda Devotees

The following letter, dated February 27th, 1955, was sent to the headquarters in Los Angeles from Yogoda Math, Dakshineswar, and signed by Prabhas Chandra Ghosh and a large representation of Yogoda members.

"The news of the death of our beloved leader, Rajarsi Janakananda, has given us a great shock. We had been looking forward eagerly to the day when we would be able to pay our respects to him here on the soil of India. It breaks our hearts to know that this, our dearest of wishes, must go unfulfilled.

"The Two Brothers, Bound by the Tie of Eternal Friendship"

"We can only submit to the will of the Divine Mother. We realize that Rajarsiji has joined Master and that the two brothers bound by the tie of eternal friendship will look after all of us.

"It was Master who taught us to love and adore Rajarsiji; his

Members attending the memorial service for Paramahansaji and Rajarsi at Yogoda Math, Dakshineswar, on March 7th, stand in silence during an intermission.

saintly life has long been before us as a great ideal. It will continue for all time to inspire travelers on the path of Self-realization.

"We are greatly encouraged by the message of your continuing loving interest in the work started by Paramahansaji in this country. May we of SRF-YSS remain indissolubly united to spread the liberating message of our beloved Masters."

"His End Was Befitting the Great Yogi that He Was"

Shortly after Rajarsiji's passing, Sri Daya Mata sent to the Dakshineswar headquarters a letter of details about the beautiful manner in which he passed. In reply, Sri Prabhas Chandra Ghosh (who had met Rajarsiji in California in 1954) said: "His has been a wonderful life, and its end was befitting the great yogi that he was."

YOGODA BRAHMACHARYA VIDYALAYA, RANCHI, INDIA (residential high school for boys, founded by Paramahansa Yogananda in 1918). Brahmachari Animananda wrote: "On March 7th we observed with great devotion the commemoration of the *mahasamadhi* of our guru, Paramahansa Yogananda; and held a service sacred to the memory of our revered late president, Rajarsi Janakananda. The meeting lasted all day, from nine-thirty in the morning until nine at night. The numerous devotees present observed fasting until *prosad* (blessed food) was distributed at three o'clock. The services started with *puja* (divine worship) and ended with *kirtan* (religious chanting). There were readings from the *Vedas* and from *Yogi Kathamrita* (Bengali edition of *Autobiography of a Yogi*). Sri Ram Kishore Roy, who presided, gave a long address on the divine lives of Paramahansaji and Rajarsiji."

In a later letter, Brahmachari Animananda, secretary, YSS Ashram, Ranchi, wrote: "I am sorry I had no opportunity to sit at Rajarsiji's feet. His life, however, teaches me the lesson of selflessness and of wholly dedicating oneself to God and Guru. Our aim should be to adore the example set by him and thereby to please our Guru, who called Rajarsiji his 'blessed, beloved, little one.'"

SANANDA LAL GHOSH, CALCUTTA, INDIA. Sananda, younger brother of Paramahansa Yogananda, and leader of the YSS Center in Calcutta, wrote: "I have just heard the heartrending news of the death of Rajarsiji. I am sure he could not bear the separation from his Master and has joined him."

Mr. Lynn in meditation, Encinitas, August 1953. He often said: "On the Path of Self-realization one feels the divine Life within him. He experiences the union of his individual soul with the universal Spirit."

TWO RARE FLOWERS IN EARTH'S GARDEN — PARAMAHANSA YOGANANDA AND JAMES J. LYNN

The Eternal Friends

(Yoganandaji and St. Lynn)

BY PRABHAS CHANDRA GHOSH
Vice-president, Yogoda Satsanga Society, Dakshineswar, India
(Written in 1937)

Paramahansaji journeyed far
Across vast lands and seas
To meet kindred spirits in the West.
The light of th' East was on his face,
A thousand mothers' love within his eyes,
All-conquering smiles upon his lips,
And in his words the ring of Realization.
On and on he moved in his quest.
As he spoke,
Truth threw off the masks of centuries
To reveal itself.
Quietly the other came,
A son of God — St. Lynn; seeking Silence
Amidst tumults of a dollar-driven age.
In tranquil communion they met.

Visions arose of the dim past
When, side by side, they had sat
On banks of the sacred Ganges,
In caves of hoary Himalayas,
To hear, within, the music of the spheres.
Oh, what meeting of two most ancient friends!
Not all the distance of Old World from the New
Nor all the vicissitudes of life
Had succeeded in keeping them apart.
Under the starry heavens, by babbling brooks,
In cliff-top hermitage 'bove Encinitas' splashing
        paradise seas,
In silence they met again and again.
Together they heard
And answered the call of th' Infinite.
Space melted; Time lost its wings;
And from the springs of united joy
Flowed a strong stream carrying waters of life
To countless souls struggling on rugged roads.
What else can these blessed travelers do
But sing His praise?
He who in divine mercy
Chose to bring His two sons
To preach His gospel together —
Love walking arm in arm with Faith,
Hope with Charity;
To dispel delusion-wraith
And perfume earth with wisdom, amity.

Guruji (*right*) holds in his hand a gift-card, whose message he reads aloud to Mr. Lynn. The beloved disciple is opening a Christmas gift from Paramahansaji. Photo taken in Guruji's study in the Encinitas hermitage, 1944.

Eulogies at Rajarsi's Funeral

The funeral service in Los Angeles, California, for Rajarsi Janaka-nanda, late president of SRF-YSS, was held at Forest Lawn Memorial-Park in the hall called "Church of the Recessional" at 10 a.m., February 23, 1955.

On this occasion Sri Daya Mata, president of SRF-YSS since March 7, 1955, gave the following moving talk.

Sri Daya Mata Tells of Rajarsi's Humility and Simplicity

Dear ones, please forgive me if my voice breaks with emotion this morning. This occasion, for us and for the world, is a solemn one. We of Self-Realization Fellowship have lost the physical presence of a beloved saint, our revered president; the world has lost one of its most eminent sons.

It was in 1932 that Master traveled to Kansas City to give a series of lectures and classes. There he met Mr. Lynn — the devotee who later became Rajarsi Janakananda. In 1933 Mr. Lynn visited the Los Angeles headquarters for the first time. An incident took place then that has remained in my memory all these years. One evening Master called me to his kitchen and asked me to bring him a needle and a spool of black thread. He was holding a pair of suspenders. When I had brought the requested articles he began to sew up a rent in the suspenders. I quickly offered to do the work, but he replied: "Oh, no, I will fix these myself. Can you imagine! Mr. Lynn has worn these same suspenders for ten years." Master was filled with delight and affection, realizing that although Mr. Lynn could have purchased almost anything, he had

A slight smile of ineffable peace was on Rajarsi's face as he lay in his casket at the funeral on Feb. 23, 1955. The pile of rose leaves (*extreme right*) was a tribute from hundreds of Self-Realization members and friends in Los Angeles who filed past the casket, dropping rose petals.

Some of the floral tributes at Rajarsi's funeral, Forest Lawn Memorial-Park, Los Angeles, Feb. 23, 1955. The beloved second president died of pneumonia on Feb. 20th in Borrego Springs.

lived so simply that one pair of suspenders had been worn and mended over a period of ten years.

This incident left an indelible impression on my mind. Truly Rajarsi was one of those great devotees who had learned to live "in the world, but not of it." His simplicity was untouched by the material success he had achieved. He was the most humble of men, his mind ever remaining fixed on God.

Two Divine Children, Strolling on the Lawn

My mind recalls another inspiring picture that I want to share with you: a picture of those two lovers of God; one the Master, one the disciple — him whom Paramahansaji called his "little one" and his "most blessed beloved little one."

During those times when Master and Rajarsi were in Encinitas together, every evening they could be seen walking, hand in hand, up and down the flagstone path on the lawn in back of the hermitage. Their eyes would be shining with the love and friendship they shared with God and with each other. We younger disciples would race to the windows at eventide to watch those two divine children as they strolled along. Sometimes Master would be speaking about some deep philosophical subject, and then his "little one" would remain quiet, listening intently. At other times both would be silent, absorbed in the inner bliss.

Seldom has the world seen such a perfect friendship. Observing them together, we were often reminded of the beautiful relationship of St. Francis and Brother Bernard.

Few men have reached the heights of material success attained by Rajarsi; fewer still, particularly in the West, have reached the great spiritual heights scaled by him. It is remarkable indeed when one man is able to ascend to the top of both those peaks!

The world will soon forget the business accomplishments of Mr. Lynn, but the name of Rajarsi Janakananda will be immortalized for the great services he rendered to Self-Realization Fellowship; and, above all, for his spiritual splendor and sweetness that helped everyone around him to realize more fully the beauty of the Divine Beloved that absorbed his whole being.

Dr. Lewis Pays Tribute to Rajarsi's Greatness

The following eulogy was delivered at Rajarsi's funeral by Rev. M. W. Lewis, vice-president of Self-Realization Fellowship

We are unable to pay adequate tribute with words to such a noble and exalted soul as James J. Lynn, known to most of us as Rajarsi Janakananda. He lived engrossed in the light and love of the Infinite Father, an illumination bestowed on him through the channel of our

SRI DAYA MATA

The Reverend Mother Daya Mata has been president and spiritual head of Self-Realization Fellowship/Yogoda Satsanga Society of India since 1955 (succeeding Rajarsi Janakananda, the second president).

beloved master Paramahansa Yogananda. Only with the language of our hearts may we pay fitting tribute to Rajarsi. And that language is the unconditional divine love we feel for him.

II Corinthians 4:18 reads: "We look not at the things which are seen, but at the things which are not seen: for the things which are seen are temporal; but the things which are not seen are eternal."

No one understood this wisdom better than our beloved Rajarsi. As proof we have his exemplary life. He was a great organizer, a keen businessman; yet in the face of present-day tensions he somehow found the time daily to merge himself in the light and love of God and his guru. Rajarsi often said: "Since meeting Master I have found the peace and bliss that supersedes all else."

In II Corinthians 5:1 we find the words: "For we know that if our earthly house of this tabernacle were dissolved, we have a building of God, an house not made with hands, eternal in the heavens." Rajarsi knew that "building of God," that "house eternal in the heavens." He once said: "I am a free soul, unlimited by the body-consciousness; I am free to roam in the all-pervading light and love of God and Master."

If Rajarsi was so free even while he was here, how much more free is he now, when the heavy earthly vehicle has been cast aside! We shall miss his physical presence, but let us rejoice in his complete freedom and in the thought that he is wholly one with his Master in God.

In I Corinthians 15:58 we read: "Therefore, my beloved brethren, be ye steadfast, unmovable, always abounding in the work of the Lord."

By establishing the Self-Realization Fellowship on a firm financial foundation and by the example of his ideal life, Rajarsi Janakananda indeed "abounded in the work of the Lord." Through his instrumentality many men will take heart and be lifted from darkness to light.

Bhagavad-Gita 18:68 reads as follows: "He who, having shown the highest devotion to Me, shall declare this supreme secret among My devotees, shall come, beyond doubt, to Me." Rajarsi was one of those great souls to whom this verse refers. By daily meditation on God, he showed Him "the highest devotion"; and by his life and good works he "declared" or proved his deep desire to share with others the "supreme secret" of man's essential divinity.

The Gita continues: "Nor is there any among men who performeth dearer service to Me than he; nor is any other more beloved by Me." How inspiring is this divine assurance that God's heart is deeply touched by a beautiful life such as Rajarsi's!

May each of us be not engulfed in this dream-world of God's, which seems unsettling — even, at times, frightening. *Let us know the Divine Dreamer.* Like our beloved Rajarsi, let us make God the eternal Polestar of our lives.

RAJARSI JANAKANANDA AND REV. M. W. LEWIS

The president and the vice-president of SRF at the hermitage, Encinitas, 1952. In a eulogy at Rajarsi's funeral, Dr. Lewis said: "By establishing Self-Realization Fellowship on a firm financial foundation and by the example of his ideal life, Rajarsi indeed 'abounded in the work of the Lord.' Through his instrumentality many men will take heart and be lifted from darkness to light."

Mr. Lynn in a lettuce patch at Lynn Farms, Borrego Springs, California, New Year's Day 1954. The 668-acre tract produces alfalfa, tomatoes, asparagus, grapes, and cantaloupes. Mr. Lynn was deeply interested in new methods for proper treatment of the soil.

The late president of Self-Realization Fellowship, who never drank or smoked, was a vegetarian for the last twenty-five years of his life. He ate cooked food only at dinner in the evenings. During the day he took fresh fruit juices and raw vegetable juices.

FATHER AND MOTHER OF JAMES J. LYNN

Jesse Williams Lynn, Scottish-Irish, was a farmer all his life. He was proud of his son James, who, when success came, bought for his parents a modern-type home in Archibald, Louisiana. Jesse Lynn died in 1945 at the age of ninety-two. Part of his obituary in the *Beacon-News,* Rayville, Louisiana, read: "His personality was one of rare sweetness and charm. His private life and his associations with neighbors and friends were models of manly virtue and of true and upright citizenship. In him were love of purity; a spirit of tenderness and kindness; Christian integrity and loyalty; loving fidelity to his family and friends; delicacy of thought and feeling; a high conception of one's work as the expression of one's character, and, therefore, a holy thing; courage to fight, even to the end, the ills of life; and a soul aglow with Southern warmth."

Beloved by All, Both Parents Had Long and Useful Lives

Salethia Jane Archibald Lynn, of Scottish blood, was born in 1855 into the family after which the town of Archibald (James' birthplace) was named. She died in 1943 at the age of eighty-eight. Extracts from her obituary in the *Beacon-News* are as follows: "She practiced her [Presbyterian] religion and consecrated her life to the welfare of others. She gave her utmost in devoted service, prompted by a heart as open as the gates of day. She shed kindness as the sun sheds light."

THE LINE OF MASTERS
BEHIND PARAMAHANSA YOGANANDA

Lahiri Mahasaya   Mahavatar Babaji   Sri Yukteswar

(An artist, with Paramahansaji's help, drew the picture of Babaji)

Mahavatar Babaji

Mahavatar Babaji revived in this age the lost scientific meditation technique of *Kriya Yoga*. In bestowing *Kriya* initiation on his disciple Lahiri Mahasaya, Babaji said, "The *Kriya Yoga* that I am giving to the world through you in this nineteenth century is a revival of the same science that Krishna gave millenniums ago to Arjuna; and that was later known to Patanjali and Christ, and to St. John, St. Paul, and other disciples."

In 1920, Mahavatar Babaji came to Yoganandaji's home in Calcutta, where the young monk sat deeply praying for divine assurance about the mission he was soon to undertake. Babaji said to him: "Follow the behest of your guru [Sri Yukteswar] and go to America.... You are the one I have chosen to spread the message of *Kriya Yoga* in the West. *Kriya Yoga,* the scientific technique of God-realization, will ultimately spread in all lands and aid in harmonizing the nations through man's personal, transcendental perception of the Infinite Father."

Lahiri Mahasaya (1828-1895), Disciple of Babaji

Lahiri Mahasaya was Babaji's chief 19th-century disciple. Though he was a man of family and business responsibilities, Lahiri Mahasaya's divine illumination attracted to him thousands of disciples in India.

Sri Yukteswar (1855-1936), Disciple of Lahiri Mahasaya

Sri Yukteswar was a disciple of Lahiri Mahasaya, and guru of Sri Yogananda. The beautiful lives of these three masters are described in *Autobiography of a Yogi.*

Sri Yogananda (1893-1952), Disciple of Sri Yukteswar

Yogananda was the first great master of India to live in the West for a long period (over thirty years). He initiated 100,000 students in Yoga, the science of spiritual development. By writing lessons and training teachers he insured the long continuance of his mission: "Yoga for the West."

Yoganandaji a Premavatar, "Incarnation of Love"

Babaji is a *Mahavatar,* "Divine Incarnation"; Lahiri Mahasaya was a *Yogavatar,* "Incarnation of Yoga"; and Sri Yukteswar was a *Jnanavatar,* "Incarnation of Wisdom."

Rajarsi Janakananda bestowed on his guru, Paramahansa Yogananda, the title of *Premavatar,* "Incarnation of Love."

CHRISTMAS CARDS, SENT TO PARAMAHANSA YOGANANDA,
HANDWRITTEN BY RAJARSI JANAKANANDA

(LEFT) Rajarsi Janakananda has written: "With my gratitude for your love and the blessings of spiritual consciousness brought to me by your love and grace and by my unconditional love for you. (*signed*) LITTLE ONE." Master often called his disciple "Little One," because of Mr. Lynn's humility. Mr. Lynn signed himself as "Little One" in nearly all his letters to Master.

(RIGHT) Rajarsi has written: "Christmas, 1941. When you melt into Divine Mother while relaxing in this chair, we pray that you take all of us with you. Divine blessings and unconditional love."

This card was attached to a Christmas gift from Rajarsi: a reclining-type chair. From time to time Master would sit in the chair, enwrapped in the peace of *samadhi* (superconsciousness). The disciples around him were awefully aware that in his presence was a shower of blessings.

A LETTER TO PARAMAHANSA YOGANANDA
IN MR. LYNN'S HANDWRITING

"I have dived deeper into God than ever before,
and wherever I go will be with Him"

Encinitas, Calif.
April 22nd [1951]

Blessed Beloved Master:

Just a short last note before my departure for Kansas City. It is difficult to realize that I must depart this holy environment and cast myself again into the busy and noisy business environment. I have dived deeper into God this time than ever before, and wherever I go will be with Him.

The dates you sent are delicious and I have eaten generously of them since they came. The variety gives me a change from the Deglet Noors [dates grown in Indio, California] although all are good and the change is welcome and enjoyed. The Deglet Noors are the best—so you and I think. Thank you for your loving thought of me.

Good-bye for a while, and with all my blessings and love,

LITTLE ONE